Music, Music, Music

S0-CNE-327

Dona Herweck Rice

Publishing Credits

Rachelle Cracchiolo, M.S.Ed., *Publisher*
Conni Medina, M.A.Ed., *Managing Editor*
Nika Fabienke, Ed.D., *Content Director*
Véronique Bos, *Creative Director*
Shaun N. Bernadou, *Art Director*
Carol Huey-Gatewood, M.A.Ed., *Editor*
John Leach, *Assistant Editor*
Courtney Roberson, *Senior Graphic Designer*

Image Credits: All images from iStock and/or Shutterstock.

Library of Congress Cataloging-in-Publication Data

Names: Rice, Dona, author.
Title: Music, music, music / Dona Herweck Rice.
Description: Huntington Beach, CA : Teacher Created Materials, [2019] |
    Identifiers: LCCN 2018029716 (print) | LCCN 2018032110 (ebook) | ISBN
    9781493899340 | ISBN 9781493898602
Subjects: LCSH: Music--Performance--Juvenile literature.
Classification: LCC ML457 (ebook) | LCC ML457 .R53 2019 (print) | DDC
    780--dc23
LC record available at https://lccn.loc.gov/2018029716

Teacher Created Materials

5301 Oceanus Drive
Huntington Beach, CA 92649-1030
www.tcmpub.com

ISBN 978-1-4938-9860-2
© 2019 Teacher Created Materials, Inc.
Printed in China
Nordica.082018.CA21800936

 like her.

Snap

 like him.

Snap

Snap

so you can be

like them.

  like her.
Blow

 like him.
Blow

Blow

so you can be

like them.

Clap

like her.

Clap

like him.

Clap

so you can be

like them.

 like her.

Tap

 like him.

Tap

Tap

so you can be

like them.

 like her.

Sing

 like him.

Sing

 so you can be

Sing

like them.

High-Frequency Words

New Words

can	her
him	like
so	them

Review Words

be	you